T0380920

A Book of Angels
Edited by D. A. F. N. Dailey

Blessed on St. JOHN OF THE CROSS's Feast day, 12/14/18, by
Father Nick Paloso (St. Timothy, San Mateo, and Our Lady of the Pillar, Half Moon Bay)
Father Gabriel Flores (St. Francis of Assisi, East Palo Alto)
Blessed on 1/16/2020 by Father Sione Malakai Katoe
(Tongan ministry, West Coast, USA)

To order additional copies of this book, contact:
Xlibris
844-714-8691
www.Xlibris.com
Orders@Xlibris.com

Cover illustration: *Choir of Angels* by Saint Sister Hildegard um Bingen (Germany, b. 1098–d. AD 1179)

Back cover illustration by Gustave Dore's *Rosa Celeste* based on Dante's *Paradiso.*

Names: Dailey, David A. F. N.

Subjects: Jesus Christ, Angels, Moses, St. Simon Peter, St. Augustine of Hippo, St. Ambrose, St. Jerome, St. Paul (Saul), St. Gregory the Great, St. Isadore of Seville, Pseudo-Dionysius the Areopagite, St. Thomas Aquinas, St. Francis de Sales, St. Catherine, St. Joan of Arc, St. Gemma Galgani, St. Pope John XXIII, St. Pope John Paul II, Pope Francis I, guardian angels, archangels, cherubim, seraphim, Thrones, Dominions, Virtues, Powers, Principalities

NIV
Scripture quotations marked NIV are taken from the Holy Bible, New International Version®. NIV®. Copyright © 1973, 1978, 1984 by International Bible Society. Used by permission of Zondervan. All rights reserved. [Biblica]

NASB
Scripture quotations marked NASB are taken from the New American Standard Bible®, Copyright © 1960, 1962, 1963, 1968, 1971, 1972, 1973, 1975, 1977, 1995 by The Lockman Foundation. Used by permission.

NKJV
Scripture quotations marked NKJV are taken from the New King James Version. Copyright © 1982 by Thomas Nelson, Inc. Used by permission. All rights reserved.

ISBN: Softcover   978-1-6698-4856-1
        Hardcover   978-1-6698-4857-8
        EBook   978-1-6698-4855-4
Library of Congress Control Number: 2022917781
Print information available on the last page

Rev. date: 10/28/2022

Book of Angels was inspired by both the editors' curiosity and knowledge of experiences documented in The Bible. Beautiful pictures are well integrated into the script.

It includes over 70 full-color illustrations and is written in English easily understandable by seventy graders. The illustrations make it appealing for all ages. The focus is on godly-angels and not those relating to the devil. In fact, the information is accurate and no false accounts or hearsay is included.

The basis comes from Roman Catholic, Eastern Orthodox, Anglican, and some Islamic sources.

The proposed cover is of the choir of angels as conceived in splendid color by St. Hildegard of Bingen from the 12th Century.

Writer and Management Consultant
• Educational Background:
Masters Degree in Public Health and Safety
Liberal Arts Bachelors from Indiana University
Certificate in Technical Writing and Communications from the University of California, Santa Cruz
• Qualifications:
-- Writer of Web-Blogs since 2008 that include religious content
-- Over 25 years as an active member of Toastmasters International – Achieved
Able Toastmaster, Gold certification

A BOOK OF ANGELS
—with *Seraphim, Cherubim, Ophanim, Archangels, and Guardian Angels*

St. Francis de Sales preached, *"Make yourself familiar with the angels, and behold them frequently in spirit; for without being seen, they are present with you."*

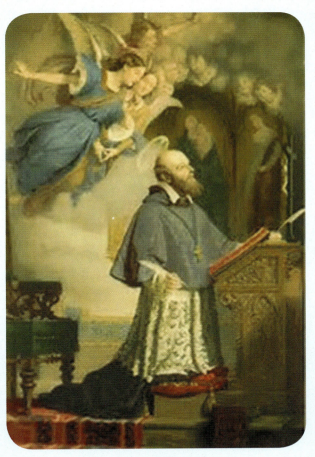

St. Francis de Sales
(1567–1622)

Intelligence and *power* are the principal attributes of angels that perform *the will of God* and praise Him.
As **messengers**, angels perform *the will of God*.
Wisdom, or **pure intelligence**, is what sets angels apart from other living beings.
This book will not discuss fallen angels but those following *the will of God*.

The editor D. A. F. N. Dailey was inspired by the works and encouragement from the following religious leaders:

✢ **Reverend Father Ed Bohnert (Archdiocese of San Francisco)**

✢ **Reverend Pastor Father Bert Chilson (Archdiocese of Denver)**

✢ **Friar Father Christopher Fadok, OP (Dominican Order)**

✢ **Pastor Dave Peterson (Presbyterian)**

✢ **Reverend Pastor Jeff Carlson (Lutheran)**

✢ **Reverend Msgr. Father John R. Coleman (St. Francis of Assisi Roman Catholic Church)**

Contents

ACKNOWLEDGMENTS AND ARTWORK

Preface

Archangels are widely recognized as God's most important angels because of their interaction with humans. It is because of these noteworthy interactions with people that archangels are the most recognizable and well-known of all nine orders of angels.

Thus, _A Book of Angels_ begins with a discussion of archangels.

Some religious texts have named seventy-two archangels of God, known as the "Angels of the Shem Hamephorash."

The Eastern Orthodox tradition mentions thousands of archangels; however, only seven archangels are venerated by name.

Many believe that Archangel Gabriel was the first major angel mentioned, by name, during the course of time in the Bible.

Some believe that another archangel, Jophiel, was present in the Garden of Eden with Adam and Eve.

Three archangels—Raphael, Michael, and Gabriel—have been recognized by the Roman Catholic Church with sainthood. All Saints' Day is celebrated on the first of November every year. There is a special feast day for these three archangels on September 29.

The anniversary honoring all guardian angels is established for October 2.

While Gabriel appears to Daniel in a dream and was present at the Annunciation to the Blessed Virgin Mary (announcing the conception of Emmanuel), there was a battle at the beginning of time (as referenced in the book of Revelation) among God and Satan, Michael the Archangel, and Lucifer. Thus, St. Michael the Archangel would be the first archangel in world history.

Enjoy this book that includes over ninety illustrations of angels.

Archangels

Michael tramples the devil underfoot, and in his left hand holds a green date-tree branch, and in his right hand a spear with a white banner (or sometimes a fiery sword), on which is outlined a scarlet cross.

Gabriel: strength (power) of God, herald and servitor of Divine omnipotence (Dan 8:16, Luke 1:26). He announces the mysteries of God...Gabriel with a branch from Paradise, presented by him to the Most Holy Virgin, or with a shining lantern in his right hand and with a mirror made of jasper in his left.

Raphael: the healing of God, the curer of human infirmities (Tobit 3:16, 12:15)...Raphael holds a vessel with healing medications in his left hand, and with his right hand leads Tobias, carrying a fish for healing (Tobit 5-8).

Uriel: the fire or light of God, enlightener (3 Ezdras 5:20). We pray for him to enlighten those with darkened minds...Uriel in his raised right hand holds a naked sword at the level of his chest, and in his lowered left hand "a fiery flame."

Selaphiel: the prayer of God, impelling to prayer (3 Ezdras 5:16). He prays to God for mankind...Selaphiel in a prayerful posture, gazing downwards, hands folded on the chest.

Jehudiel: the glorifying of God, encouraging exertion for the glory of the Lord and interceding for the reward of efforts...Jehudiel holds a golden crown in his right hand, in his left, a whip of three red (or black) thongs.

Barachiel: distributor of the blessings of God for good deeds, entreats the mercy of God for people...Barachiel is shown with a white rose on his breast.

Jeremiel: the raising up to God (3 Ezdras 4:36)...Jeremiel holds balance-scales in his hand.

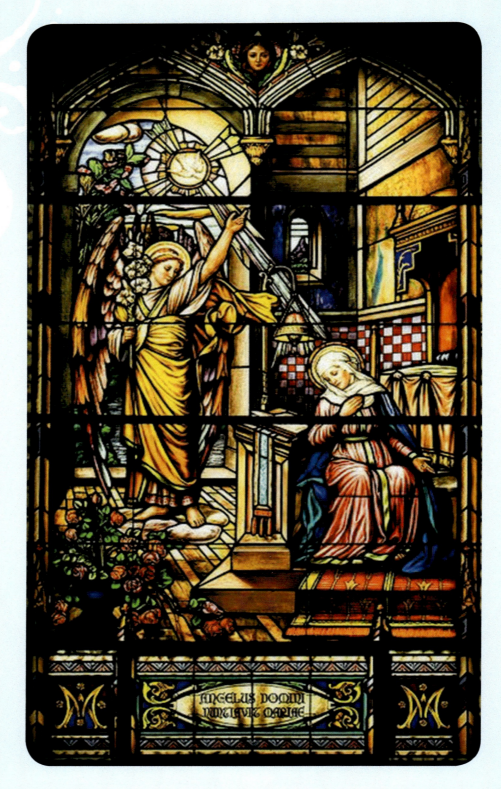

Archangel Gabriel appears to Mary at the Annunciation.

Archangel Michael was the leader of the army of angels fighting for the good of God against Satan/Lucifer and his legion of fallen angels.

St. Michael the Archangel defeats the Devil.

The Angelic Council
St. Jehudiel, St. Gabriel, St. Selatiel, St. Michael, St. Uriel,
St. Rafael, and St. Barachiel (beneath is the mandora of Jesus
Christ and blue Cherubim angels and a red Seraphim angel)

In various writings, seven archangels are designated to each day of the week:

- Michael (Sunday)
- Gabriel (Monday)
- Raphael (Tuesday)
- Uriel (Wednesday)
- Selaphiel (Thursday)
- Jegudiel (Friday)
- Barachiel (Saturday)

A fresco of Uriel (c. AD 200) in Cairo, Egypt

Seasons of the Year

It has been written that the seasons are ruled by four archangels: spring is Raphael, summer is Uriel, fall is Michael, and winter is Gabriel.

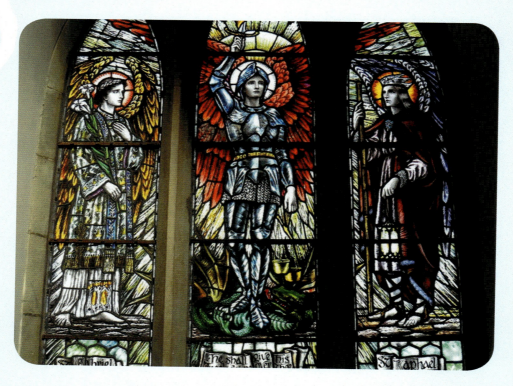

Archangels Gabriel, Michael, and Rafael

Following this line of reasoning, Aries (astrologically ruled by Mars) represents spring, Cancer (ruled by Moon) represents summer, Libra (ruled by Venus) represents autumn, and Capricorn (ruled by Saturn) represents winter. Therefore, by association, Raphael is Mars, Uriel is Moon, Michael is Venus, and Gabriel is Saturn.

The Eastern Orthodox tradition venerates seven archangels: Michael, Gabriel, Rafael, Uriel, Selaphiel, Jegudiel, and Barachiel. Jeremiel (an eighth archangel) is sometimes included.

Seven archangels around the Christ Child and Mary

Michael

The name of Michael in the Hebrew language means "Who is like God" or "Who is equal to God." The Archangel St. Michael has been depicted from earliest Christian times as a commander, who holds in his right hand a spear with a red cross and a linen ribbon, with which he attacks Lucifer/Satan, and in his left hand a green palm branch.

The Archangel Michael is especially considered to be the guardian of the Orthodox faith and a fighter against heresies.

Archangel Michael statue on display at the University of Bonn

The Archangel St. Michael has four main roles or offices.[1]

His **first role** is the leader of the Army of God and the leader of heaven's forces in their triumph over the powers of hell. He is viewed as the angelic model for the virtues of the *spiritual warrior*, with the conflict against evil at times viewed as the *battle within*.

The second and third roles of Michael deal with death.

In his **second role**, Michael is the angel of death, carrying the souls of all the deceased to heaven. In this role, Michael descends at the hour of death and gives each soul the chance to redeem itself before passing, thus consternating the devil and his minions. Catholic prayers often refer to this role of Michael.

In his **third role**, he weighs souls in his perfectly balanced scales. For this reason, Michael is often depicted holding scales.

In his **fourth role**, St. Michael, the special patron of the Chosen People in the Old Testament, is also the guardian of the Church. It was thus not unusual for this angel to be revered by the military orders of knights during the Middle Ages. Thus, the nomenclature of villages around the Bay of Biscay reflects that history.

St. Michael the Archangel

---

1 . New King James Version (NKJV), Sounds True, 2007.

Gabriel

Gabriel means "God is my strength" or "Might of God." He is the herald of the mysteries of God, especially the incarnation of God and all other mysteries related to it.

Archangel Gabriel is depicted as follows: In his right hand, he holds a lantern with a lighted taper inside, and in his left hand, a mirror of green jasper. The mirror signifies the wisdom of God as a hidden mystery.

**Archangel Gabriel, icon from the Byzantine Era (c. 1387–1395)
on display at the Tretyakow Gallery**

Raphael

Raphael means "It is God who heals" or "God heals" (reference in Tobit 3:17 and 12:15, NASB). Raphael has been depicted leading Tobit (who is carrying a fish caught in the Tigris River) with his right hand and holding a physician's alabaster jar in his left hand.

The Archangel Raphael

Raphael helps on a round trip between Nineveh and Media, unites Sarah to marry Tobiah, chases off the evil Asmodeus, returns with Tobit's funds from Media, and cures Tobit's blindness. After returning and healing the blind Tobit, Azarias makes himself known as "the angel Raphael, one of the seven, who stand before the Lord" (Tob. 12:11–22, NASB).

Archangel Raphael with Tobias

The Gospel of John speaks of the pool at Bethesda, where many ill people rested, awaiting the moving of the water.

"An angel of the Lord descended at certain times into the pond; and the water was moved. And he that went down first into the pond after the motion of the water was made whole of whatsoever infirmity he lay under" (John 5:1–4, NIV).

Because of the healing powers often linked to Raphael, the angel spoken of is generally associated with St. Raphael, the Archangel.

Uriel

Uriel stained glass window in the cloisters of Chester Cathedral

Uriel means "God is my light" or "Light of God" (II Esdras 4:1 and 5:20, NKJV). He is depicted holding a sword against the Persians in his right hand and a flame in his left.

The Fourth Book of Esdras, which mentions the angel Uriel was popular in the West was frequently quoted by Church Fathers, especially Ambrose, during the fourth century in Italy, but was never considered part of the Roman Catholic biblical canon.

The book of Enoch, which presents itself as written by Enoch, mentions Uriel in many of the component books. In chapter 9 which is part of *The Book of the Watchers* (second century BCE), only four angels are mentioned by name. These four are Michael, Uriel, Raphael, and Gabriel (though some versions have a fifth angel: Suryal or Suriel). However, the later chapter 10 lists the name and function of seven angels. It is Uriel, one of the holy angels, who is over the world and over Tartarus (hell).

**Uriel mosaic at St. John's Church in Boreham, Wiltshire,
by James Powell and Sons of the Whitefriar's Foundry**

The Book of the Angels explains that Uriel, Raphael, and Gabriel were present before God to testify on behalf of humankind. The archangels wish to ask for divine intervention during the reign of the Fallen Gregori (also known as the Fallen Watchers). These fallen take human wives and produced half-angel, half-human offspring called the Nephilim.[2]

Uriel is responsible for warning Noah about the upcoming Great Flood.

Then said the Most High, the Holy and Great One spoke, and sent Uriel to the son of Lamech, and said to him: "Go to Noah and tell him in my name 'Hide thyself!' and reveal

---

2 . Mashafa Mala'ekt (Book of Angels) Haymanot Falasha text based on the first part of the Apocalypse of Paul.

to him the end that is approaching: that the whole earth will be destroyed, and a deluge is about to come upon the whole earth, and will destroy all that is on it."[3]

Uriel discusses the fate of the leaders of the Nephilim and the fallen ones:

"And Uriel said to me: 'Here shall stand the angels who have connected themselves with women, and their spirits assuming many different forms are defiling mankind and shall lead them astray into sacrificing to demons "as gods," (here shall they stand) till the day of the great judgment in which they shall be judged till they are made an end of.

'And the women also of the angels who went astray shall become sirens.' And I, Enoch alone, saw the vision, the ends of all things; and no man shall see as I have seen."[4]

Uriel then acts as a guide for Enoch for the rest of the Book of Watchers that make up First Enoch.

The archangel is discussed within the Second Book of Esdras found in the biblical Apocrypha (called Esdras IV in the Vulgate). Uriel is sent for instruction after the prophet Ezra asks God a series of questions. According to the Revelation of Esdras, the angels that will rule at the end of the world are Michael, Gabriel, Uriel, Raphael, Gabuthelon, Beburos, Zebulon, Aker, and Arphugitonos. The last five listed only appear in this book and nowhere else in apocryphal or apocalyptic works.[5]

Uriel, on the right with a red cloak, in the *Virgin of the Rocks* (Louvre version) by Leonardo da Vinci, 1483–86

---

3 . Ibid.
4 . Mashafa Mala'ekt (Book of Angels) Haymanot Falasha text based on the first part of the Apocalypse of Paul.
5 . 2 Esdras, New King James Version Bible (NKJV), 1992 Edition.

In the rescue of Jesus's cousin, John the Baptist, from the Massacre of the Innocents ordered by King Herod, Uriel plays a role. The archangel carries John and his mother St. Elizabeth to join the Holy Family after their flight into Egypt. Their reunion is depicted in Leonardo da Vinci's painting *Virgin of the Rocks*.

During the lives of Adam and Eve, Uriel is thought to be present. He is regarded as the spirit and one of the cherubs in the third chapter of Genesis. He may have been one of the angels who helped bury Adam and Abel in paradise.

In addition to a cherub, he is recognized as an angel representing repentance. Uriel appears as the Angel of Repentance in the <u>Apocalypse of Peter</u>, who is graphically represented as being as pitiless as any demon.

Uriel "stands at the garden of Eden with a fiery revolving sword" (Gen. 3:24, OJB) or as the angel who "watches over thunder and terror."

Archangel Uriel has also become known as the Angel of Sunday (*Jewish Encyclopedia*, Enoch 20:2, OJB), the Angel of Poetry, and one of the Holy Sephiroth arising from medieval Jewish mystical traditions.

Uriel is the archangel who checked the doors of Egypt for lamb's blood during the plague. He also holds the key to the Pit during the End Times and led Abraham to the West.[6]

Uriel is often depicted carrying a book or a papyrus scroll representing wisdom. Uriel is a patron of the arts.

Uriel **by Leonardo DaVinci**

In addition to being a patron of arts, Uriel is known as an Angel of Presence, Prince of Presence, Angel of the Face, Angel of Sanctification, and Angel of Glory. A Prince of the Presence is an angel who is allowed to enter the presence of God.

A scriptural reference to an angel of presence is found in Isaiah 63:9, NIV:

> In all their affliction he was afflicted, and the angel of his presence saved them: in his love and in his pity he redeemed them; and he bare them, and carried them all the days of old.

---

6 . *Jewish Encyclopedia*, studylight.org, 1901.

The Anglican intercessional prayer to St. Uriel the Archangel is as follows:

O holy Saint Uriel, intercede for us that our hearts may burn with the fire of the Sacred Heart of Jesus.

Assist us in cooperating with the graces of our confirmation that the gifts of the Holy Spirit may bear much fruit in our souls.

Obtain for us the grace to use the sword of truth to pare away all that is not in conformity to the most adorable Will of God in our lives, that we may fully participate in the army of the Church. Amen.[7]

---

7 . "Our Patron Saint," www.urielsg.org.

Sealtiel

Sealtiel (also known as Selaphiel) means "Request of God" and "Intercessor of God." He is depicted with his face and eyes lowered, holding his hands on his bosom in prayer.

It is possible that he was the Angel of the Lord who stopped Abraham from sacrificing Isaac (Gen. 22:12, NKJV).

Sealtiel has a special interest in meditation, contemplation, and worship.

Some Christian traditions consider Selaphiel as the angel in Revelation 8:3–4 (NASB) of the Bible who presents the prayers of people on earth to God in heaven:

Another angel, who had a golden censer, came and stood at the altar.

He was given much incense to smoke of the incense, together with the prayers of God's people, went up before God from the angel's hand.

Sealtiel/Selaphiel

In the Catholic tradition, he is depicted as a thurifer, one who carries the incense.

When depicted in iconography by himself or with individual characteristics, he is shown in an attitude of humble prayer, with downcast eyes and arms crossed over his breast. He is also sometimes seen kneeling with incense in a thurifer, praying.

Prayer is considered his special attribute.

Prayer is the most difficult thing to achieve, and one must be instructed in it. Let us pray to Archangel Salaphiel for the Lord to grant us this gift of divine prayer.

Jegudiel

Titles of "the Glory of God," "God of the Jews," "Laudation of God" and "Glorifier of God" are given to Jegudiel. He is depicted bearing a golden wreath in his right hand and a triple-thonged whip in his left hand.

He is often depicted in iconography holding a flaming crown of salvation and a three-thonged whip in hand, which symbolizes reward from God for the righteous and punishment for the sinners. The classic Eastern Orthodox depiction usually shows him standing upright, holding a crown in his right hand and a rod or staff in his left hand.

St. Jegudiel

Jegudiel

Prayers

A prayer to Jegudiel as the Patron Saint of Hard Work and Leadership is as follows:

St. Jegudiel the Archangel, angel of praise to God, pray for us, that in every act, in every job, in every work, and in every labor we may constantly carry out the will of the Lord gladly and in praise for all He has given us. Amen.

A prayer to Jegudiel as the Patron Saint of God's Mercy follows as:

O merciful Archangel, St. Jegudiel, dispenser of God's eternal and abundant Mercy. Because of our sinfulness, we do not deserve God's forgiveness. Yet He continually grants us forbearance freely and lovingly. Help us in our determination to overcome our sinful habits and be truly sorry for them. Bring each one of us to true conversion of heart. That we may experience the joy of reconciliation which it brings, without which neither we, as individuals, nor the whole world can know true peace. Thou who dost continually intercede for us, listen to our prayers. Present to God the Father all of these petitions. We ask this through our Lord Jesus Christ, He who lives and reigns with the Father, in the unity of the Holy Spirit, one God, forever and ever. Amen.[8]

---

8 . "The Rational Heavenly Powers," Russian Orthodox Church, 2010.

Barachiel

"God's Blessings" and "Blessed by God" are the meanings of Barachiel's name. He is often pictured holding roses against his breast. Barachiel pleads for the mercy of God and passes along the blessings of God for good deeds.

The archangel Barachiel is described as one of the angelic princes of the Third Heaven, with a myriad of some 496,000 ministering angels attending him; this is described in the Third Book of Enoch. He is described in the Almadel, the Lesser Key of Solomon, as one of the chief angels of the first and fourth chora. Interestingly, he is regarded as the angel of hail and lightning.[9]

Barachiel means "Blessings of God."

If not shown holding a white rose against the chest, his cloak is covered with rose petals. The scattering of rose petals symbolizes and represents God's sweet blessings showering down on people. In Roman Catholicism, Barachiel is depicted holding a bread basket or a staff; both symbolize the blessings of the lives of children that God bestows on their parents.

---

9 . EOTB, the Ethiopian Orthodox Tewahedo Church Bible.

St. Barachiel holding an abundant basket

Barachiel

Described as ruler of the order of Seraphim, Brachiel is one of the angels who serves as great and honored angelic princes in heaven. Barachiel leads 496,000 angels, who attend and assist him. He is considered one of the seraphim class of angels who guard God's throne, as well as the leader of all the guardian angels.

Jeremiel

Jeremiel (a.k.a. Jerahmeel, Eremiel, Remiel) means "God's exaltation" and "God's mercy." He is venerated as an inspirer and awakener of exalted thoughts that raise a person toward God (II Esdras 4:36 and 3 Esdras 4:32, EOTB). Jeremiel is sometimes included as the eighth archangel.

Within the text of the deuterocanon of the Ethiopian Orthodox Tewahedo Church, it describes him as one of the angels that watch over "the spirits that sin in the spirit" (1 Enoch 20:7–8, EOTB).

Jeremiel

Note that the Catholic Church gives no official recognition to the names given in some apocryphal sources, such as Raguel, Saraqael, and Remiel (<u>Book of Enoch</u>) or Izidkiel, Hanael, and Kepharel.

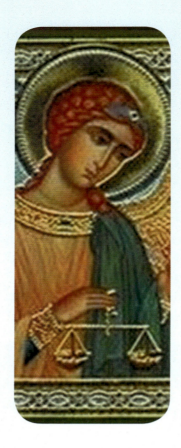

Jeremiel

====

Per quoted references from St. Francis de Sales (b. 1567 in Thorens-Glieres, France, and became the bishop of Geneva, Switzerland, in 1602):

> LIVE JESUS! Yes, my beloved sisters and daughters, I say the words with intense delight: LIVE JESUS in our memory, in our will, and in our actions! Have in your thoughts only Jesus, in your will have only the longing for his love, and in your actions have only obedience and submission to his good pleasure by an exact observance of the Rule, not only in externals, but much more, in your interior spirit: a spirit of gentle cordiality toward one another . . .

We are sometimes so busy being good angels that we neglect to be good men and women.[10]

---

10 . St. Jeanne-Françoise de Chantal (Francis de Sales) *Letters of Spiritual Directions*, Paulist Press, 1988.

Nine Orders in the Choir of Angels

According to St. Augustine of Hippo, "Angel" is the name of their office, not of their nature.

If you seek the *name of their nature, it is "spirit";*
if you seek the **name of their office**, it is "angel":
from what they *are, "spirit,"*
from what they **do**, "angel."[11]

St. Augustine (c. AD 395) by Peter Paul Rubens (c. 1610)

11 . Augustine of Hippo, *Enarrationes in Psalmos.*

Rosa Celeste
Circling the abode of God from Dante's Divine Comedy *Paradiso*
as illustrated by Gustave Dore

"THE CHOIR OF ANGELS"

Christian theology places seraphim in the highest choir of the angelic hierarchy. They are the caretakers of God's throne, continuously singing "holy, holy, holy."

Pseudo-Dionysius the Areopagite in his <u>Celestial Hierarchy</u>, written during the fifth century, drew upon the book of Isaiah in fixing the fiery nature of seraphim in the medieval imagination.

Seraphim in his view helped the deity maintain perfect order and are not limited to chanting the *trisagion*—*"Holy God, Holy Mighty One, Holy Immortal One, have mercy on us."*

Taking his cue as well from writings in the Rabbinic tradition, the author gave an etymology for the *seraphim* as "those who kindle or make hot":

> The name *seraphim* clearly indicates their ceaseless and eternal revolution about Divine Principles, their heat and keenness, the exuberance of their intense, perpetual, tireless activity, and their elevated and energetic assimilation of those below, kindling them and firing them to their own heat, and wholly purifying them by a burning and all-consuming flame; and by the unhidden, unquenchable, changeless, radiant and enlightening power, dispelling and destroying the shadows of darkness.[12]

---

12 . Pseudo-Dionysius Areopaita, <u>*De Coelesti Hierarchia.*</u>

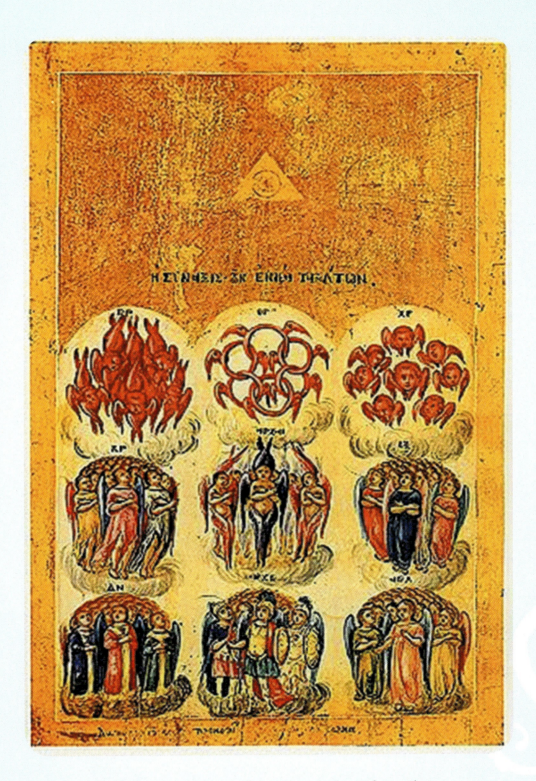

An Orthodox icon of the Nine Orders of Angels:
Seraphim—Thrones—Cherubim
Dominations—Virtues—Powers
Principalities—Archangels—Angels

St. Thomas Aquinas's *Summa Theologica* (written between the years 1265–1274) follows the *Celestial Hierarchy*, written by St. Augustine centuries beforehand, in dividing the angels into three hierarchies, each of which contains three orders, based on their proximity to God, corresponding to the nine orders of angels.

- Seraphim, Cherubim, and Thrones
- Dominations, Virtues, and Powers
- Principalities, Archangels, and Angels (including Guardian Angels)

These nine orders of angels were formally recognized by Pope St. Gregory I. Gregory the Great's papacy began in 590 and lasted until 604 at the age of sixty-four.

St. Thomas Aquinas worked tirelessly, studying and writing.

St. Thomas Aquinas girded by angels *Temptation of St. Thomas Aquinas*, painting by Diego Rodriquez de Silva y Velazquez (c. 1650)

SPECIAL MESSENGER ANGELS

Metatron, a leading seraphim is not mentioned in the Hebrew Bible, nor is it mentioned in the early Enoch literature. How the name originated is a matter of debate. It is believed that God created the angel when Enoch died (Gen. 5:24, NKJV).

Although Metatron is mentioned in a few brief passages in the Talmud, he appears primarily in mystical Kabbalistic texts within the Rabbinic literature. In that tradition, he is the highest of the angels and serves as the celestial scribe or "recording angel."[13]

Jophiel is believed to be a close friend of Metatron.
Jophiel is believed to have guarded the Tree of Knowledge in the Garden of Eden.
Jophiel is believed to have expelled Adam and Eve.

---

13 . R. Travers Herford, *Christianity in Talmud and Midrash*, Williams & Norgate, 1903.

Jophiel is believed to have looked after Noah's three sons.
Sources say that Jophiel is the ruler of fifty-three legions of the order of Thrones.
Jophiel's name means "the Beauty of God."

Some sources state Jophiel is one of the leaders of cherubim. Jophiel is in charge of the cherubim, particularly the Shemhamphorasch angels Haziel, Aladiah, Lauviah, Hahaiah, Iezalel, Mehahel, Hariel, and Hakamiah.

Jophiel is said to be able to help anyone who calls upon her to absorb information, bring order to thoughts, and provide artistic and intellectual inspiration.

Engraving (c. 1610–1637) of Jophiel by Crispijn van de Passe

The angel Jophiel (Hebrew meaning "Beauty of God," "Divine Beauty"), also called Iophiel, Iofiel, Jofiel, Yofiel, Youfiel, Zophiel (*Tsophiel* "spy of God," "watchman of God"), and Zuriel (*Tsuriel* "my rock is God").

Jophiel is the archangel of (1) wisdom, (2) understanding, and (3) judgment. He is listed as one of the seven archangels in Pseudo-Dionysian teachings.

On the following page is Francesco Botticini's *The Assumption of the Virgin*.

A vast, dramatic scene of heaven and earth has been conceived by Botticini.

Jesus Christ blessing the Blessed Virgin Mary (BVM) is revealed as a dome-shaped gate of heaven.

Surrounded by ranks of neat orders of angelic beings, saints, and Old Testament figures, she kneels as his earthly mother.

The ranks include an aging couple, Adam and Eve, beneath mother and the Son of Man.

The ancestors of the human race are pictured wearing camel-skin robes.

Six-winged red seraphim, the four-winged blue cherubim, and below them, the cherubic-like Thrones are beneath Jesus and the BVM. The circular Ophanim (Thrones) were called this because they were the carriers of God's throne.

Angels of the second order—the Dominions, Virtues, and Powers—rule the lower angels, the planets and humankind.

Painted under the second order of angels are the angelic beings most associated with the earth, the principalities; the archangels, who deal with military and commercial matters; and the angels, all God's messengers to humankind. Among the angels are saints and Old Testament figures.

The immortal BVM has ascended into heaven after her death to join this place pictured full of clouds and golden light. Her empty tomb below has been filled with lilies, to the amazement of the apostles who gather around it.

The image is based upon a poem by a contemporary of Francesco Botticini—the Florentine apothecary and writer Matteo Palmieri—whose image is shown kneeling to the left of the tomb, opposite Botticini's wife Niccolosa.

**The Assumption of the Virgin Mary among the nine choirs
of angels (c. 1470) by Francesco Botticini**

THE FIRST ORDER (TRIAD) OF ANGELS

There is a hierarchy of angels, including three spheres, each with three distinct kinds. The highest three are the first order. These angels are the closest in proximity to God's throne. The first order/sphere of angels serve as the heavenly servants of God the Son incarnated.

- Seraphim
- Cherubim
- Ophanim, also known as Thrones

Thrones of angels delighting God.

Seraphim, Angels Closest to God

**Seraphim surround the divine throne from the
fourteenth-century *Petites Heures de Jean de Berry***

Seraphim (singular "seraph") is literally translated "burning ones"; the word seraph is normally a synonym for serpents when used in the Hebrew Bible. Described in Isaiah 6:2–7 (NASB), seraphim are the highest angelic class, and they serve as the caretakers of God's throne and continuously shout praises:

"Holy, holy, holy is the Lord of hosts; the whole earth is full of his glory!"

According to Isaiah, the seraphim are described as fiery six-winged beings; with two wings, they cover their faces, with another two they cover their feet, and the last two they use to fly.

Every seraph has a fiery passion for doing God's good works.

Pseudo-Dionysius the Areopagite (AD fifth century), in his *Celestial Hierarchy*, drew upon the book of Isaiah in fixing the fiery nature of seraphim in the medieval imagination. Seraphim, in his view, helped the deity maintain perfect order.

The name seraphim clearly indicates their ceaseless and eternal revolution about *Divine Principles*, their heat and keenness, the exuberance of their intense, perpetual, and tireless activity, and their elevated and energetic assimilation of those (angels) below.

Seraphim are kindling themselves and firing them with their own heat and wholly purifying them by a burning and all-consuming flame and by the unhidden, unquenchable, changeless, radiant, and enlightening power, dispelling and destroying the shadows of darkness.

**Angels of the Highest Sphere/Triad/Order:
Cherub—Seraph—and Ophanim**

St. Thomas Aquinas in his *Summa Theologiae* (thirteenth century) offers a description of the nature of seraphim:

> The name "Seraphim" does not come from charity only, but from the excess of charity, expressed by *The Word* and fire. Hence Dionysius expounds the name "Seraphim" according to the properties of fire, containing an excess of heat.

Now in "fire," we may consider three things:

1. **First** is their movement. Seraphim move upward and continuous. This signifies that they are borne inflexibly toward God.

2. **Secondly,** the active force is "heat," which is not found in fire simply, but exists with a certain sharpness, as being of most penetrating action, and reaching even to the smallest things, and as it were, with superabundant fervor.

   This "heat" is signified by the action of these angels, exercised powerfully upon those who are subject to them, rousing them to a like fervor, and cleansing them wholly by their heat.

3. **Thirdly,** consider in fire the quality of clarity or quality of brightness.

   The third quality signifies that these angels have in themselves an inextinguishable light and that they also perfectly enlighten others.

Cherubim—
ANGELS WITH SPECIAL PURPOSES

Cherubim have six wings and four faces (Isa. 6:1–7 and Ezek. 1:5–24, NIV):

One of a **man**
An **ox** on the left
A **lion** on the right
An **eagle** (later adopted as the symbols of the four evangelists Matthew, Mark, Luke, and John)

Cherubim angels have six conjoined wings covered with eyes, a lion's body, and the feet of oxen. One pair modestly covers their lower bodies, a second pair veils their faces, and the third pair of wings are prepared to fly.

The cherubim are mentioned in eight books in all versions of the Bible:

- Genesis 3:24, NKJV: "So He drove the man out and at the east of the garden of Eden. He stationed the **cherubim** and the flaming sword which turned every direction to guard the way to the tree of life."

- Exodus 25:17–22, NASB: "And the (gold) **cherubim** shall stretch forth their wings on high."

- Numbers 7:89, NKJV: "Moses heard the voice of One speaking to him from above the mercy seat that was on the ark of the Testimony, from between the two **cherubim**."

- 2 Samuel 6:2, NKJV: "The Lord of Hosts, who dwells between the **cherubim**."

- 2 Chronicles 3:7–14, NASB: "For the Most Holy Place he made a pair of sculptured **cherubim** and overlaid them with gold."

- Ezekiel 10:12–14 and 28:14–16, NKJV: "You were anointed by a guardian **cherub**, for so I ordained you."

- 1 Kings 6:23–28, NKJV: "He placed the (gold) **cherubim** inside the innermost room of the temple."

- Revelation 4:6–8, NASB: "Day and night they never stop saying: 'Holy, holy, holy is the Lord God Almighty, who was, and is, and is to come.'"

Modern English usage has blurred the distinction between cherubim angels and cute *putti*. *Putti* are often depicted as the wingless human baby/toddler-like beings traditionally used in figurative art.

by Leon Brazile Perrault (1882)

Cherubim as described by Ezekiel.

Cherubim have four faces: one of a man, an ox, a lion, and an eagle (these were later adopted as the symbols of the four evangelists Matthew, Mark, Luke, and John). They have six conjoined wings covered with eyes, a lion's body, and the feet of oxen.

The writers of the four gospels are represented on a cherub with the head of a man (St. Matthew), the lion's head (St. Mark), the head of a lamb (St. Luke), and the head of an eagle (St. John).

No. 30.

No. 38.
S. Matthew.

No. 34.

No. 31.

No. 39.
S. Mark.

No. 35.

No. 32.

No. 40.
S. Luke.

No. 36.

No. 33.

No. 41.
S. John.

No. 37.

The Four Evangelists

Cherubim guard the way to the tree of life in the Garden of Eden (Gen. 3:24, NKJV).

Cherubs also guard the throne of God, which is often referred to as the holy mountain of God (Ezek. 28:14–16, NIV).

Ophanim

These angelic princes of the first order of angels are often also called "Ofanim, Wheels of Galgallin." It is said that they were the actual wheels of the Lord's Heavenly Chariot (Merkabah). "The four wheels had rims and they had spokes, and their rims were full of eyes round about." They are also frequently referred to as "many-eyed ones."

Depiction of Ezekiel's vision of the Ophanim

The "thrones," also known as "ophanim" (offanim) and "galgallin," are creatures that function as the actual chariots of God driven by the cherubs. They are characterized by peace and submission; God rests upon them.

Thrones are depicted as great wheels containing many eyes and reside in the area of the cosmos where material form begins to take shape.

Ophanim (references: 1 Peter 3:21–22, NASB; Daniel 7:9, NKJV; Ezekiel 1:13–23, NIV; Revelation 20:4, NKJV; and Colossians 1:16, NASB), who are carriers and guards of the throne of God, never sleep.

St. Peter writes that these angels are in heaven in submission to God with the resurrected Jesus Christ at His right hand.

St. Paul's letter to the Colossians states that God created thrones through Him and for Him.

Daniel's description of his dream reports that God's throne was like a fiery flame with wheels of burning fire.

Ophanim chant glorias to God and remain forever in his presence. They mete out divine justice and maintain the cosmic harmony of all universal laws.

Ophanim

The name of the most glorious and exalted Thrones denotes that which is exempt from and untainted by any base and earthly thing and the supermundane ascent up the steep.

For these have no part in that which is lowest, but dwell in fullest power, immovably and perfectly established in the Most High, and receive the Divine Immanence above all passion and matter, and manifest God, being attentively open to divine participations.

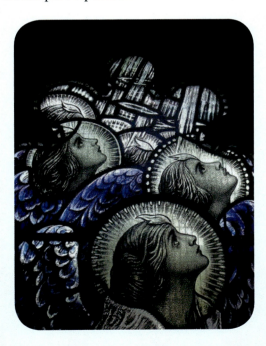

Thrones worshiping God.

Ophanim

SECOND ORDER OF ANGELS

Angels of the Second Sphere (Second Triad or Order) work as heavenly governors of the creation by subjecting matter and guiding and ruling the spirits.

- Dominions or lordships
- Virtues or strongholds
- Powers, also known as authorities

**Second Order of Angels
Dominions—Strongholds—Powers**

Dominions or Lordships

The "Dominions" (Eph. 1:21, NKJV; Col. 1:16, NASB) (Lat. *dominatio*, plural *dominationes*, also translated from the Greek term *kyriot* as "lordships") or "Dominations" are presented as the hierarchy of celestial beings "Lordships" in some English translations of the *De Coelesti Hierarchia*.

The Dominions regulate the duties of lower angels. It is only with extreme rarity that the angelic lords make themselves physically known to humans.

Zadquiel is one of the chiefs of the Dominions.

These angels of the Dominions lord over the lower choirs of angels and humanity.

The Dominions look like divinely beautiful humans with a pair of feathered wings. They may be distinguished by wielding orbs of light at the top of their scepters or on the pommel of their swords.

Dominions

Dominions

They, lordships, take illumination from the hierarchies and govern the universe.

VIRTUES OR STRONGHOLDS

The angels of the Strongholds are those through which signs and miracles are made in the world of Christian angelology.

The Virtues run the operation of movement in the universe. In St. Thomas Aquinas's *Summa Theologica*, they are presented in the celestial choir.

Two men in white apparel were alongside Jesus Christ when he ascended into heaven (Acts 1:10–11, NASB). The two are thought to be members of the choir of Virtues.

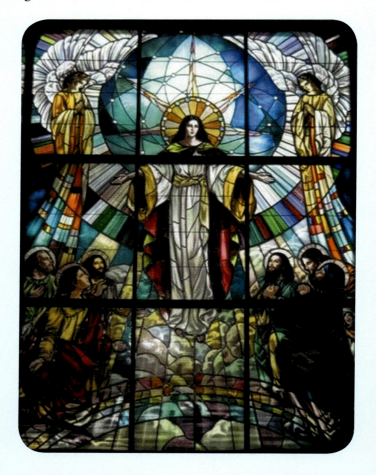

Jesus Christ's ascension into heaven among Virtues

Ascension into Heaven

These Strongholds are often associated with planets, chemical elements, the four seasons, and nature. Virtues are often depicted with a golden belt and a lily or red rose symbolizing the passion of Christ.

Their term appears to be linked to the attribute "might" from the Greek root *dynamis* in Ephesians 1:21, which is also translated as "Virtue" or "Power." They are presented as the celestial choir "Virtues" in the *Summa Theologica* written by Thomas Aquinas.

Archangel Michael is the prince regent of the choir of Virtues. Gabriel and Raphael are also princes of the same order of Strongholds.

Virtues

From Pseudo-Dionysius the Areopagite (fifth century AD):

The name of the holy Virtues signifies a certain powerful and unshakable virility welling forth into all their Godlike energies; not being weak and feeble for any reception of the divine Illuminations granted to it; mounting upwards in fullness of power to an assimilation with God;

Never falling away from the Divine Life through its own weakness, but ascending unwaveringly to the superessential Virtue which is the Source of virtue: fashioning itself, as far as it may, in virtue; perfectly turned toward the Source of virtue, and flowing forth providentially to those below it, abundantly filling them with virtue.[14]

---

14 . Pseudo-Dionysius the Areopagite, _De Coelesti Hierarchia._

POWERS OR AUTHORITIES

The "Powers" (Latin *potestas* (f), pl. *potestates*), or "Authorities," from the Greek *exousiai*, plural of *exousia* (see Greek root in Ephesians 3:10, NKJV). The primary duty of the "Powers" is to supervise the movements of the heavenly bodies in order to ensure that the cosmos remains in order.

Both terms "powers" and "authorities" are written in 1 Peter 3:22 (NIV).

The angels of the powers choir of angels assist God in governing the natural order. The powers are tasked with fighting the war against evil and the demonic choirs.

Being warrior angels, they also oppose evil spirits, especially those that make use of the matter in the universe, and often cast evil spirits to detention places. These angels are usually represented as soldiers wearing full armor and helmet and also having defensive and offensive weapons such as shields and spears or chains respectively.

First Colossians 1:16 (NASB) states,

> For in Him were created all things in heaven and on earth,
> the visible and invisible,
> whether thrones or dominions or
> principalities or powers;
> all things were created through Him and for Him.

The powers are the bearers of conscience and the keepers of history. They are also the warrior angels created to be completely loyal to God. Some believe that with the only exception of Satan, no power has ever fallen from grace. Satan was the chief of the powers before he fell into hell (see also Ephesians 6:12, NKJV).

The duty of the authorities are to oversee the distribution of power among humankind, hence their name.

There are many times in the Old Testament of angels appearing to the Israelites in the midst of military battles. These occurred from before the fall of Jericho (Josh. 5:13–15, NIV) to the defeat of Nicanor's army in 161 BC (Macc. 15:17–28, NASB).

Chamuel—Prince of the Seraphim and Chief of the Order of Powers

Chamuel, a prince of the seraphim, has been mentioned as the chief of the order of powers. Chamuel is thought to be the angel that wrestled with Jacob for a full night (Gen. 32:24–30, NKJV). Although the comforting angel for Jesus in the Garden of Gethsemane is believed to be Gabriel, it may have been Chamuel.

THE THIRD SPHERE OF ANGELS

The third order/triad are angels who function as heavenly guides, protectors, and **messenger**s to human beings. These angels interact with and serve humanity closely.

- Principalities, also known as rulers
- Archangels
- Angels of the third sphere of Christian angelic hierarchy—guardian angels

Principalities—Rulers

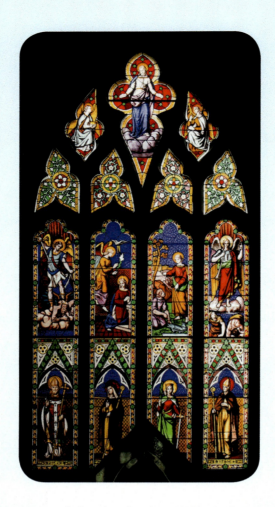

Messengers of the third sphere of angels in action

Principalities or Rulers

The "principalities" (Latin: *principati*), also translated as "princedoms" and "rulers," from the Greek *archai*, plural of *arch* (see Greek root in Ephesians 3:10), are the angels that guide and protect nations, or groups of peoples, and institutions such as the Church.

In order for angels to perform their divine ministry successfully, the principalities preside over the bands of angels and charge and direct them. There are some who administer and others who assist.

The rulers are the princes of the lowest triad of angels that are assigned to care and guard communities, kingdoms, political states, and Christian parishes and churches.

As written in Deuteronomy 32:8 (NKJV), "Each nation has its own guardian."

The principalities are shown wearing a crown and carrying a scepter.

Principality Angel

The principality angels' duty also is said to be to carry out the orders given to them by the upper-sphere angels and bequeath blessings to the material world. Their task is to oversee groups of people. They are the educators and guardians of the realm of earth. Like beings related to the world of the *germinal ideas*, they are said to inspire living things to many things, such as art or science.

St. Paul used the term *rule* and *authority* in Ephesians 1:21 (NASB) and *rulers* and *authorities* in Ephesians 3:10 (NASB).

Principality angel

Guardian Angels:
PROTECTION AND INTERCESSION WITH GOD

A guardian angel is one that is assigned to protect and guide a particular person, group, kingdom, or country. Belief in guardian angels can be traced throughout all antiquity. The concept of tutelary angels and their hierarchy was extensively developed in Christianity in the 5th century by Pseudo-Dionysius the Areopagite.

The theology of angels and tutelary spirits has undergone many refinements since the 5th century. Belief in both the East and the West is that guardian angels serve to protect whichever person God assigns them to, and present prayer to God on that person's behalf.[15]

In the New Testament the concept of guardian angel may be noted. Angels are everywhere the intermediaries between God and man; and Christ set a seal upon the Old Testament teaching:

"See that you despise not one of these little ones: for I say to you, that their angels in heaven always see the face of my Father who is in heaven." (Matthew 18:10 - NASB).

A twofold aspect of the doctrine is here put forth: even little children have guardian angels, and these same angels lose not the vision of God by the fact that they have a mission to fulfill on earth.

---

15 . *Catechism of the Catholic Church*, Section 336.

Guardian Angel **by Pietro da Cortona (1656)**

Barachiel is also the chief of the guardian angels.

Personal guardian angels are not of a separate order but rather come from the order of angels. It is a common belief that they are assigned to every human being, Christian or not.

The "angels" (or *malakhim*, the "plain" angels, *angelos*, i.e., messenger or envoy) are the lowest order of the angels and the most recognized.

They are the ones most concerned with the affairs of living things. Within the category of the angels, there are many different kinds, with different functions. The angels are sent as messengers to humanity. Personal guardian angels come from this class.

In addition to the angel who succored Christ in the garden of Gethsemane, there is another example in the New Testament. It was the angel who delivered St. Peter from prison.

In Acts 12:12–15 (NASB), after Peter had been escorted out of prison by an angel, he went to the home of "Mary the mother of John, also called Mark." The servant girl, Rhoda, recognized his voice and ran back to tell the group that Peter was there. However, the group replied, "It must be his angel."

With this scriptural sanction, Peter's angel was the most commonly depicted guardian angel in art and was normally shown in images of the subject, most famously Raphael's fresco of the *Deliverance of Saint Peter* in the Vatican.

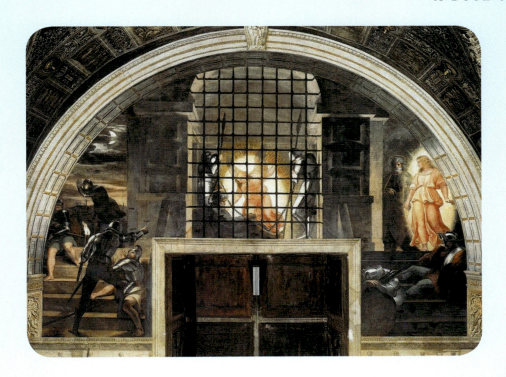

Raphael's deliverance of St. Peter

The liberation of St. Peter from prison

Hebrews 1:14 (NKJV) states, "Are they not all ministering spirits, sent to minister for them, who shall receive the inheritance of salvation?" In this view, the function of the guardian angel is to lead people to the kingdom of heaven.

According to St. Jerome, in the fourth century, the concept of guardian angels is in the "mind of the Church." He stated, "How great the dignity of the soul, since each one has from his birth an angel commissioned to guard it."

The first Christian theologian to outline a specific scheme for guardian angels was Honorius of Autun in the twelfth century. He said that every soul was assigned a guardian angel the moment it was put into a body.

Scholastic theologians augmented and ordered the taxonomy of angelic guardians. St. Thomas Aquinas agreed with Honorius and believed that it was the lowest order of angels who served as guardians, and his view was most successful in popular thought.

Then the thirteenth- and fourteenth-century Franciscan theologian John Duns Scotus (born in Scotland and lived in England, France, and Germany) stated that any angel is bound by duty and obedience to the Divine Authority to accept the mission to which that angel is assigned. He postulated that since angels have no material bodies, they could be in two different places at the same time and angels can be different from one another.

In the fifteenth century, the Feast of Guardian Angels (October 2) was added to the official calendar of Catholic holidays.

In his March 31, 1997, *Regina Caeli* address, Pope Saint John Paul II referred to the concept of guardian angel and concluded the address with the statement: "Let us invoke the Queen of angels and saints, that she may grant us, supported by our guardian angels, to be authentic witnesses to the Lord's paschal mystery."

In his October 2, 2014, homily for the Feast of Guardian Angels, Pope Francis told those gathered for daily Mass to be like children who pay attention to their "traveling companion."

"No one journeys alone and no one should think that they are alone," Pope Francis said.[16]

During the Morning Meditation in the chapel of Santa Marta, the Pope noted that oftentimes, we have the feeling that "I should do this, this is not right, be careful." This, he said, "is the voice of" our guardian angel."

"According to Church tradition," Pope Francis said, "we all have an angel with us, who guards us." The pope instructed each, "Do not rebel, follow his advice!" The pope urged that this "doctrine on the angels" not be considered "a little imaginative." It is rather one of "truth."

It is "what Jesus, what God said: 'I send an angel before you, to guard you, to accompany you on the way, so you will not make a mistake.'"

Pope Francis concluded with a series of questions so that each one can examine his/her own conscience: "How is my relationship with my guardian angel? Do I listen to him? Do I bid him good day in the morning? Do I tell him: 'guard me while I sleep?' Do I speak with him? Do I ask his advice? . . . Each one of us can do so in order to evaluate 'the relationship with this angel that the Lord has sent to guard me and to accompany me on the path, and who always beholds the face of the Father who is in heaven.'"

***

There was an old Irish custom that suggested including in bedtime prayers a request for the Blessed Mother to tell one the name of their guardian angel, and supposedly within a few days, one would "know" the name by which they could address their angel.

***

An old Dominican tradition encouraged each novice to give a name to their guardian angel so that they could speak to him by name and thus feel closer and more friendly with him.

***

There is a similar Islamic belief in the *Mu'aqqibat* (angels), also called *al hafathah*, written in the Qur'an. The Mu'aqqibat are charged with bringing blessings from the sun and taking the good deeds of men to heaven. Muhammad is reported to have said that every man has ten guardian angels. They protect man from the harm of evil jinn and shaytan angels, who keep people from death until its decreed time.

---

16 . The Guardian, Pope Francis, October 2014.

According to many Muslims, each person has two guardian angels, in front and behind him, perhaps taking turns maintaining every being in life, sleep, death, or resurrection.[17]

Angels (Arabic: ملائك *Malāʾikah*) are mentioned many times in the Qur'an and hadith. Islam is clear on the nature of angels in that they are messengers of God. They have no free will and can do only what God orders them to do. An example of a task they carry out is that of testing individuals by granting them abundant wealth and curing their illness. Believing in angels is one of the six articles of faith in Islam.

Some examples of angels in Islam:[18]

- Jibrail: the archangel Gabriel (Jibra'il or Jibril) is an archangel who serves as a messenger from God.
- Michael, or *Mikail*, is the angel of nature.
- Azrael is Azraa-eel (عزرائيل or *Izrail*), the Angel of Death. No authentic reference of this in Quran or Hadeeth. Only referenced as angel of death or ملك الموت.
- Israfil (Arabic: إسرافيل *Isrāfīl, Israfel,* meaning "the Burning One") is the angel of the trumpet in Islam, though unnamed in the Qur'an.

Along with Michael, Gabriel and Azrael, Isafil is one of the four Islamic archangels. Israfil will blow the trumpet from a holy rock in Jerusalem to announce the Day of Resurrection. The trumpet is constantly poised at his lips, ready to be blown when God so orders.

- Darda'il: the angels who travel in the earth searching out assemblies where people remember God's name.
- Kiraman and Katibin: the two angels who record a person's good and bad deeds.
- Mu'aqqibat: a class of guardian angels who keep people from death until their decreed time.
- Munkar and Nakir: the angels who test the faith of the dead in their graves. They ask the soul of the dead person questions. If the person fails the questions, the angels make the man suffer until the Day of Judgment. If the soul passes the questions, he will have a pleasant time in the grave until the Day of Judgment.
- Ridwan: the angel in charge of maintaining *jannat,* otherwise known as paradise.
- Maalik: the angel who *keeps* or *guards* hellfire.
- Harut and Marut (Arabic: هاروت وماروت) are two angels mentioned in the second Surah of the Qur'an, who were sent down to test the people at Babel or Babylon by performing deeds of magic. The Qur'an indicates that although they warned the Babylonians not to imitate them or do as they were doing, some members of their audience failed to obey and became sorcerers, thus damning their own souls.

---

17 . Quran 13:11.
18 . Quran Surah Ar-Ra'd with English translation.

More about Angels as Guardians

According to St. Thomas Aquinas, "On this road man is threatened by many dangers both from within and without, and therefore as guardians are appointed for men who have to pass by an unsafe road, so an angel is assigned to each man as long as he is a wayfarer."[19]

By means of an angel, God is said to introduce images and suggestions leading a person to do what is right.

Our guardian angels can act upon our senses (*Summa Theologica* 111:4) and upon our imaginations (*Summa Theologica* 111:3) not, however, upon our wills, except "per modum suadentis," viz. by working on our intellect and thus upon our will, through the senses, and the imagination (*Summa Theologica* 106:2 and 111:2).

The guardian angel is the patron saint of Fondachelli-Fantina in Sicily where it is celebrated also the second Sunday of July (as well as the Feast of Santissimi Angeli Custodi) when it is carried in the streets of their town.

In Genesis 18–19 (NKJV), angels not only acted as the executors of God's wrath against the cities of the plain, but they also delivered Lot from danger.

In Exodus 32:34 (NIV), God said to Moses, "My angel shall go before thee." At a much later period, we have the story of Tobias, which might serve for a commentary on the words of Psalm 91:11: "For he will command his angels concerning you to guard you in all your ways" (Ps. 33:8, 34:5, NIV).

The belief that angels can be guides and intercessors for men can be found in Job 33:23–6 (NKJV); and in Daniel 10:13 (NASB), angels seem to be assigned to certain countries. In this latter case, the "prince of the kingdom of Persia" contends with Gabriel. The same verse mentions "Michael, one of the chief princes."

***

Sergi Bulgakov writes that the Eastern Orthodox Church teaches the following:

> Each man has a guardian angel who stands before the face of the Lord. This guardian angel is not only a friend and a protector, who preserves from evil and who sends good thought; the image of God is reflected in the creature—angels and men—in such a way that angels are celestial prototypes of men.[20]

> Guardian angels are especially our spiritual kin. Scripture testified that the guardian ship and direction of the elements, of places, of peoples, of societies, are confided to the guardian angels of the cosmos, whose very substance adds something of harmony to the elements they watch over.

---

19 . Lawrence Lovasik, *Friendship With the Angels*, 2004.
20 . Sergei Bulgakov, *The Orthodox Church* (St. Vladimir's Seminary Press, 1988).

As such, before the Eastern Orthodox liturgy of the communion of the faithful, a prayer asks "for an angel of peace, a faithful guide, a guardian of our souls and bodies, let us entreat the Lord. Amen."

St. Gregory surrounded by angels

These doctors, scholars of the Church, wrote about angels:

- St. Ambrose, fourth century[21]
- St. Jerome, fourth century[22]
- St. Pope Gregory the Great, sixth century[23]
- St. Isidore of Seville in seventh century
- John of Damascus in *De fide orthodoxa*, eighth century

St. Hildegard of Bingen, Germany, had visions of God and compiled them in a book entitled, *Scivias*. She lived virtually her entire life in convents, yet was widely influential within the Church. She was chosen as abbess of her community and implemented many improvements.

On the following page is artwork by St. Hildegard (b. 1098, d. 1179), abbess of Bingen, Germany.

---

21 . James Loughlin, *The Catholic Encyclopedia* (St. Ambrose, 1907).
22 . St. Jerome, *Britannica Encyclopedia*, 2017.
23 . Gilbert Huddleston, "Pope St. Gregory the Great," *The Catholic Encyclopedia*, 1909.

Choir of Angels **by Hildegard of Bingen, eleventh century St. Sister Hildegard was widely influential within the Roman Catholic Church.**

Her importance went beyond the mystic as she advised kings and popes.

Stone statue of Hildegard

St. Hildegard wrote poems and hymns and produced treatises in the fields of medicine, theology, and natural history. St. Hildegard was an outstanding musician and artist.

***

The Reverend Donald Schneider, a learned ordained Lutheran priest, wrote that the concept of a guardian angel is found in Psalm 91, which includes a verse stating, "For [God] will command his angels concerning you to guard you in all your ways. On their hands they will bear you up, lest you strike your foot against a stone." He states that Martin Luther may have based Morning Prayer and Evening Prayer found in the _Small Catechism_ on this text, as these prayers include the supplication "Let your holy angel be with me, that the evil foe may have no power over me."[24]

***

St. Thomas Aquinas (1225–1274) and Dante Alighieri in the _Divine Comedy_ (1308–1321) made significant contributions explaining angels during the Middle Ages.

In 1567, Pope Pius V proclaimed St. Thomas Aquinas as a doctor (scholar) of the Church.

St. Pope Pius V

In the Bible, this doctrine involving angels is clearly discernable and its development well marked. In Genesis 28–29 (NKJV), angels not only act as the executors of God's wrath against the cities of the plain, but they also deliver Lot from danger. In Exodus 12–13 (NIV), _an angel_ is the appointed leader of the host of Israel; and in Exodus 32:34 (NIV), God says to Moses, "_My angel_ shall go before thee."

***

At a much later period, there is the story of Tobias, which might serve for a commentary on the words of Psalm 90:11 (NKJV): "For he hath given _his angels_ charge over thee; to keep thee in all thy ways." As well as Psalm 34:8 (NKJV): "The _angel of the Lord_ who encamps with them, delivers all who fear the Lord."

24 . Donald Schneider, "Of Guardian Angels," Faith Lutheran Church—Missouri Synod, 2013.

Psalm 91 (NASB) speaks of the security under God's protection:

> *For God commands the angels to guard you in all your ways. With their hands they shall support you, lest you strike your foot against a stone. You shall tred upon the asp and the viper, trample the lion and the dragon.*

Following St. Stephen's oration with an enthralled audience, he sees heaven and many angels prior to his death (Acts 7:1–60, NASB). Stephen was the first recorded Christian martyr about the year AD 50.

In Acts 7:55–56 (NASB), St. Stephen was filled with the Holy Spirit and reported, *"I see the heavens opened and the Son of Man standing at the right hand of God."*

St. Stephen sees God and His angels.

Malachi 3:16 (NASB) speaks of a record book maintained by angels with the names of those who righteously fear the Lord.

In 2 Maccabees 3:25 (NASB), a gold armored angel arrives to attack evil Heliodorus, who intended to profane the temple. Later in this story, 2 Maccabees 10:29 (NASB), the prayerful are aided by five golden horsemen from heaven who surround Maccabeus in battle.

Prior to another battle (2 Maccabees 11:6–8, NASB), after praying to send a good angel to combat Lysias's eighty thousand solders to save Israel, a white-clothed horseman with gold weapons appeared to lead them successfully. Finally, as described in 2 Maccabees 15:23 (NASB), they prayed to send a good angel to spread the fear of God and dread before Nicanor's army. God answered them by defeating over thirty-five thousand.

***

During the life of Jesus Christ, he described in "The Parable of the Lost Sheep" (Matt. 18:10, NIV):

> See that you do not despise one of these little ones, for I say to you that *their angels* in heaven always look upon the face of my heavenly Father.

As described in Luke 22:43 (NIV), the Father sent an angel to strengthen Jesus during his agony in the Mount of Olives garden.

An Angel comforts Christ during His agony in the garden.

During the imprisonment of Christ's apostle Peter (Acts 12:7–15, NASB), an angel was sent to free him. Refer to paintings on page 89, 90, and 106.

St. Paul in his letter mentions angels in Hebrews 1:4–14 and 13:2 (NKJV). His message of encouragement speaks to the majesty of God in concert with the angels and urges believers to welcome angels and practice hospitality and love for others.

Angels coming to aid humanity and help the needy and sick

The Rev. Dr. John W. Hanner, a Methodist minister and theologian, wrote on the topic of guardian angels in his *Angelic Study*, stating the following:

> Perhaps every Christian has a guardian angel. It may be that there is one angel to every Christian, or a score of them; or one may have charge of a score of Christians.

> Some of the ancient fathers believed that every city had a guardian angel, while others assigned one to every house and every man. None of us know how much we are indebted to angels for our deliverance from imminent peril, disease, and malicious plots of men and devils.

> Where the pious die, angels are to carry the soul to heaven, though it be a soul of a Lazarus.

An angel is a spiritual being superior to humans in power and intelligence. Angels are typically described as benevolent, dreadful, and endowed with wisdom and knowledge of earthly events, but not infallible; for they strive with each other, and God has to make peace between them.

Most angels serve either as intermediaries between heaven and earth or as guardian spirits. They are studied in the theological doctrine of angelology. In Christian science, the word *angel* is used to refer to an inspiration from God.

The use of the term has extended to refer to artistic depictions of the spirits, and it is also used figuratively to refer to messengers and harbingers and to people who possess high qualities of goodness, purity, selflessness, intelligence, or beauty.

***

Daniel is the first biblical figure to refer to individual angels by name, mentioning Gabriel (God's primary messenger) in Daniel 9:21 (NIV) and Michael (the holy fighter) in Daniel 10:13 (NIV). These angels are part of Daniel's apocalyptic visions and are an important part of all apocalyptic literature. One could explain the development of this concept of angels: "In the postexilic period, with the development of explicit monotheism, these divine beings—the 'sons of God' who were members of the Divine Council—were in effect demoted to what are now known as 'angels', understood as beings created by God, but immortal and thus superior to humans."

Daniel protected by the Angel of the Lord (French artwork from the thirteenth century)

In the book of Daniel 4:13, 17, and 23 (NKJV), there are three references to the class of "watcher, holy one" (watcher, Aramaic `*iyr*; holy one, Aramaic *qaddiysh*). The term is introduced by Nebuchadnezzar, who said he saw "a watcher, a holy one come down (singular verb) from heaven." He describes how in his dream the watcher says that Nebuchadnezzar will eat grass and be mad and that this punishment is "by the decree of the Watchers, the demand by the word of the Holy Ones" . . . "the living may know that the Most High rules in the kingdom of men." After hearing the king's dream, Daniel considers for an hour and then responds:

An angel of the Lord helps Tobias heal a blind man
by Bernardo Strozzi (reference: Book of Tobit)

In the early stage, the Christian concept of an angel characterized the angel as a messenger of God. Later came identification of individual angelic messengers: Gabriel, Michael, Raphael, and Uriel. Then in the space of a little more than two centuries (from the third to the fifth), the image of angels took on definite characteristics both in theology and in art.

Credit is due to the theological study and writings of the early doctors of the Church: Pseudo-Dionysius the Areopagite (first century AD);[25] St. Ambrose[26] (AD 374–397); St. Jerome[27] (until AD 420); St. Augustine of Hippo (until AD 430);[28] and St. Pope Gregory the Great (AD 590–604).[29]

Although angels have greater knowledge than men, they are not omniscient. God is omniscient. As Matthew 24:36 (NASB) points out when God speaks about the second coming of the Son of Man,

But of that day and hour, no one knows, neither *the angels of heaven*, nor the Son, but the Father alone.

25 . Dionysius, Saints & Angels, Catholic Online, 2019.

26 . James Loughlin, "St. Ambrose," *The Catholic Encyclopedia*, 1907.

27 . St. Jerome, *Britannica Encyclopedia*, 2017.

28 . Church Fathers, <u>City of God</u>, Book XIX, St. Augustine, New Advent, 2018.

29 . Gilbert Huddleston, "Pope St. Gregory the Great," *The Catholic Encyclopedia*, 1909.

Powers, Angels, and Dominions

ANGELIC ENCOUNTERS

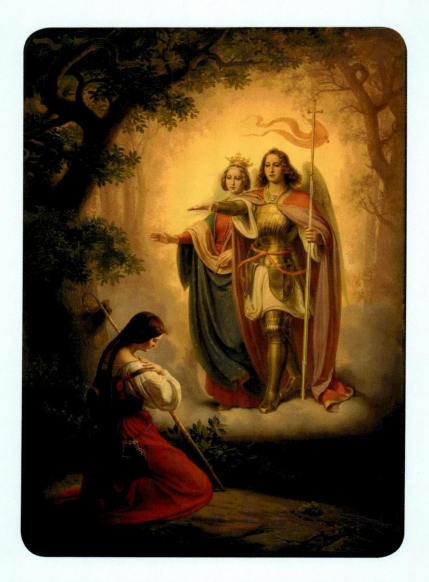

St. Catherine and Archangel Michael visit Joan of Arc (Jeanne la Pucelle d'Orleans) in 1425

The New Testament includes many interactions and conversations between angels and humans. For instance, three separate cases of angelic interaction deal with the births of John the Baptist and Jesus Christ (Luke 1:11, Luke 1:26, and Luke 2:10, NASB).

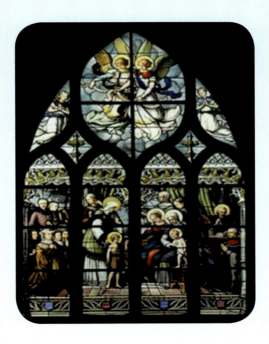

Angels present when John the Baptist first meets Jesus

In 1751, Michael the Archangel had a private revelation with the Carmelite nun Antonia d'Astonac. Sister Antonia reported that the archangel had indicated in an apparition that he would like to be honored and God glorified by the praying of nine special invocations.

These nine invocations correspond with petitions to the nine choirs of angels and are the origins of the Chaplet of Saint Michael.

Praying the chaplet, similar to reciting the rosary prayers, is believed to provide the assistance from St. Michael the Archangel and the company of one angel from each of the nine celestial choirs when approaching Holy Communion.

Carmelite Order nun Antonia d'Astonac

The Chaplet of St. Michael the Archangel begins with an act of contrition. Then there are nine salutations, one for each choir of angels. Each salutation is followed by an Our Father and three Hail Marys. Then four Our Fathers, with each honoring Archangel Michael, Gabriel, Raphael, and one's personal guardian angel are prayed.

The chaplet concludes with a prayer to Saint Michael:

> St. Michael the Archangel, defend us in battle, be our defense against wickedness and snares of the devil. May God rebuke him, we humbly pray; and do thou, O Prince of the Heavenly Host, by the power of God, thrust into hell Satan and the other evil spirits who prowl about the world for the ruin of souls. Amen.[30]

In 1851, Pope Pius IX approved the Chaplet of St. Michael based on St. Antonia d'Astonac's eighteenth-century encounter with the archangel.

In addition, for those who would recite the chaplet daily, St. Michael promised his continual assistance and that of all the holy angels during one's life. Praying the chaplet is also believed gradually to defeat demons and grant one a "pure heart," thus delivering one's soul from purgatory after mortal death. These blessings extend to the direct family.

In a biography of St. Gemma Galgani, written by the Venerable Germanus Ruoppolo, Galgani stated that she had spoken with her guardian angel.

In the early stage, the Christian concept of an angel characterized the angel as a messenger of God. Later came identification of individual angelic messengers: Gabriel, Michael, Rafael, and Uriel. Then in the space of a little more than two centuries (from the third to the fifth), the image of angels took on definite characteristics both in theology and in art.

According to St. Augustine, "'Angel' is the name of their office, not of their nature. If you seek the name of their nature, it is 'spirit'; if you seek the name of their office, it is 'angel': from what they are, 'spirit', from what they do, 'angel.'"

Basilian Father Thomas Rosica says, "Angels are very important, because they provide people with an articulation of the conviction that God is intimately involved in human life."

By the late fourth century, the Church Fathers agreed that there were different categories of angels, with appropriate missions and activities assigned to them. There was, however, some disagreement regarding the nature of angels. Some contended that angels had physical bodies while some maintained that they were entirely spiritual.

Some theologians had proposed that angels were not divine but on the level of immaterial beings subordinate to the Trinity (Father, Son, and Holy Ghost). The resolution of this Trinitarian dispute included the development of doctrine about angels.

The angels are represented throughout the Christian Bible as spiritual beings intermediate between God and men: "You have made him [man] a little less than the angels" (Ps. 8:4–5, NKJV). The Bible describes the function of angels as "messengers" but does not indicate when the creation of angels occurred.

Christians believe that angels are created beings, based on as follows: "Praise ye Him, all His angels: praise ye Him, all His hosts" (Ps. 148:2–5, NKJV); "for He spoke and they were made. He commanded and they were created" (Col. 1:16, NASB).

The Fourth Lateran Council in 1215 declared that the angels were created beings.

The council's decree, *Firmiter Credimus*, affirmed both that angels were created and that men were created after them. The First Vatican Council in 1869 repeated this declaration in *Dei Filius*, which is known as the dogmatic constitution on the Roman Catholic faith.

During the thirteenth century, St. Thomas Aquinas draws a connection of angels to Aristotle's metaphysics in his *Summa Contra Gentiles Theologica* and in *De Substantiis Separatis*, a treatise on angelology.

Although angels have greater knowledge than men, they are not omniscient like God, the Gospel of Matthew points out in 24:36 (NASB).

St. Pope John Paul II emphasized the role of angels in Catholic teachings in his 1986 address titled *"Angels Participate in History of Salvation."* He suggested that modern mentality should come to see the importance of angels.

According to the Vatican's *Congregation for Divine Worship and Discipline of the Sacraments*, "The practice of assigning names to the Holy Angels should be discouraged, except in the cases of Gabriel, Raphael and Michael whose names are contained in Holy Scripture."

Liberation of St. Peter from prison

Forget not to show love unto strangers: for thereby some have entertained angels unawares.

(Heb. 13:2)

INTERACTION WITH ANGELS DOCUMENTED IN THE BIBLE

Old Testament

In Genesis 16:7–9 (NKJV), an **angel of the Lord** found Hagar in the desert wilderness and told her to "go back to thy mistress (Sarai) and submit to her will."

**An Angel of the Lord appearing to Hagar
by Nicolas Colombel (1644–1717)**

In Genesis 19 (NASB), two **angels** led Lot, Abraham, and their family out of Sodom before its and Gomorrah's destruction.

Within Genesis 22:11–18 (NKJV), the **angels of the Lord** appear to Abraham, and the passage refers to God in the first person. The Lord's messenger stops Abraham as he is about to offer his son Isaac's life as validation of his strong faith in God.

An Angel appears to Abraham by Juan DeValdes Leal

Abraham visited by angels

God's **messengers** are seen going up and down a ladder (which popularly becomes known as Jacob's Ladder) between heaven and the promised land in one of Jacob's dreams (Gen. 28:12, NKJV). From this dream experience, the grandson of Abraham and son of Isaac, Jacob is convinced that Bethel in Canaan is the most holy land.

83

In Genesis 32:23–31 (NKJV), Jacob spent one night alone along a riverside during his journey back to Canaan and wrestled with an **angel** until daybreak.

Jacob is very anxious anticipating opposition from his twin brother Esau. He is returning with his wives, many children, and huge flocks of sheep, goats, cattle, camels, and other livestock after spending fifteen years living the land where their mother Rebekah and Jacob's wives were born—Aram Naharaim.

Jacob Wrestling with an Angel **by Gustave Dore**

Within Exodus chapter 3, NIV, the **angel of the Lord** in a brazen fire flaming out of a bush appears to Moses in verse 2. While tending a flock of sheep, he moves toward it to get a closer look, and God converses directly with Moses from the burning bush in verses 4–22.

As written in Numbers 22:22–38 (NKJV), the **angel of the Lord** meets the prophet Balaam. It is Balaam's ass that he is riding, not Balaam, who first notices the **angel** blocking the road. The ass turns into a field and begins talking to his rider about why he is getting hit. Only after they return to the road, Balaam finally recognizes the **angel** and speaks to him about delivering the word of God. He promises to continue his journey and only say what the angel of God tells him.

The Angel of the Lord Meets Balaam on his donkey—Nuremberg Chronicles (1493)

In Judges 2:1–3 (NIV), the **angel of the Lord** appears to the children of Israel. They are threatened for their infidelities and not following their covenant with God.

Within Judges 6:11–13 (NASB), an angel announces to Gideon that he is to save his people although Gideon fears for his life because he was in the presence of God. The **angel** proclaims, "The Lord is with you, O Champion!"

In Judges 13:3–7 (NKJV), the **angel of the Lord** appears to Manoah and his barren wife, foretelling the birth of Samson, who would ultimately deliver the Israelites from the power of the Philistines.

**An Angel of the Lord appears to Manoah
by Eustache LeSueur (c. 1640).**

Isaiah 63:9, NKJV, mentions the Angel of Presence, which some theologians believe could have been Uriel the Archangel.

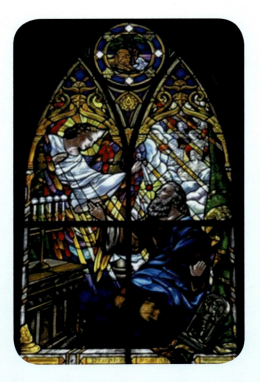

An Angel appears to the great Prophet Isaiah.

A scriptural reference to an Angel of Presence in Isaiah 63:9, NIV:

In all their affliction he was afflicted, and the angel of his presence saved them: in his love and in his pity he redeemed them; and he bare them, and carried them all the days of old.

Earlier in the book of Isaiah (Isaiah 6:2-7, NASB), the prophet is called by the Lord. Isaiah is greeted by vivid visions of seraphim.

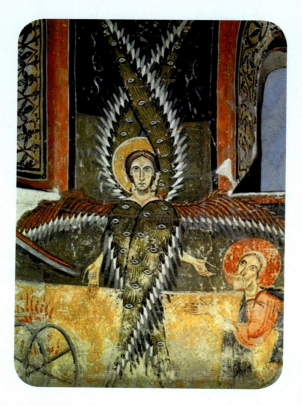

**Seraphim touches the lips of Isaiah with an ember
from God's altar and purges his sin (Isaiah 6:6).**

Recorded within chapter 1 of the book of Ezekiel are his visions of seraphim, cherubim, and thrones of angels.

***

The accounts of Daniel's dreams involving **Archangel Gabriel** are documented in Daniel 8:16 and 9:21, NKJV. Gabriel provides valuable instructions.

Angels saving Daniel's life inside the den of lions is described in both Daniel 6:23 and 14:33, NKJV.

Daniel was able to provide King Nebuchadnezzar interpretation of his dreams due to his vision of "a holy sentinel" that came down from heaven (Dan. 14:10–14, NIV).

In Daniel 3:49–90, NIV, it is written that Azariah and his two companions did not die in the king's fiery furnace because of an **angel of the Lord**. The angel aided the faithful by driving out the flames and making a dew-laden breeze blow through the furnace.

***

The great prophet Elijah was saved by God through the works of an angel. Two appearances of the same angel are documented in 1 Kings 19:5–8, NKJV. After one day of traveling through the desert to flee the murderous fate of other prophets, exhausted Elijah took rest under a broom tree and begged the Lord to take his life. After he fell asleep, an **angel** woke him and urged him to eat and drink from a jug of water and hearth cake he brought. Hours later, the **angel** interrupted Elijah's rest and ordered him to eat more.

Elijah was able to nourish his body well enough to complete a forty-day-and-night trip to safety at the sacred mountain of God, Horeb. From there, Elijah was able to live many years and complete his mission of prophecy and the will of God.

***

The book of Zechariah (c. 520 BC) documents the **angel of the Lord** in two instances. In Zechariah 1:12, NASB, the angel pleads with God for mercy on behalf of Jerusalem and the cities of Judah. Then the angel speaks to Zechariah: "Proclaim: Thus says the Lord of hosts, 'I am deeply moved for the sake of Jerusalem and Zion, and I am exceedingly angry with the complacent nations; whereas I was but a little angry, they added to the harm.' Therefore, says the Lord: 'I will turn Jerusalem in mercy; My house shall be built in it and a measuring line shall be stretched over Jerusalem.' Proclaim further: Thus says the Lord of hosts: 'My cities shall again overflow with prosperity; the Lord will again comfort Zion, and again choose Jerusalem.'"

After rebuking Satan and taking away the sin of the high priest, the **angel of the Lord** speaks to Joshua and others (Zechariah 3:4–10, NASB). The angel offered God's reassurance: "Thus says the Lord of hosts: 'If you walk in my ways and heed my charge, you shall judge my house and keep my courts, and I will give you access . . . On that day, you will invite one another under your vines and fig trees.'"

Jacob's Ladder
Referenced in Genesis 28:10–19

New Testament

The New Testament includes many interactions and conversations between angels and humans. For instance, three separate cases of angelic interaction deal with the births of John the Baptist and Jesus Christ.

In Luke 1:11 (NASB), an *angel* appears to Zechariah to inform him that he and Elizabeth will have a child despite their old age, thus proclaiming the birth of John the Baptist.

In Luke 1:26–38 (NASB), Archangel Gabriel visits the Virgin Mary in the Annunciation to proclaim the immaculate conception and foretell the birth of Jesus Christ.

Annunciation

Visitation of Mary with Elizabeth as referenced in Luke 1:39–56, NASB

The third event is the appearance of angels to the shepherds announcing the birth of Jesus Christ. It says in Luke 2:9, NKJV:

And all at once an **angel of the Lord** came and stood by them, and the glory of the Lord shone about them, so that they were overcome with fear.

An Angel announces Emmanuel's birth to the shepherds

Matthew 1:20 (NASB) accounts the first time that an **angel** comes to St. Joseph in a dream, saying, "Joseph, son of David, do not fear to take Mary as you wife, for that which is conceived in her is from the Holy Spirit."

St. Joseph is visited a second time by an angel as written in Matthew 2:13 (NASB): "Behold, an **angel of the Lord** appeared to Joseph in a dream and said, 'Rise, take the child and his mother, and flee to Egypt, and remain there until I tell you, for Herod is about to search for the child, to destroy him.'" Later when King Herod died, it is written in Matthew 2:19 (NASB): "Rise, take the child and his mother and go to the land of Israel, for those who sought the child's life are dead."

Angel appears to Joseph by Daniele Crespi

According to Matthew 4:11 (NKJV), Jesus spent forty days in the desert after his baptism in the River Jordan. Satan's battles were fierce but "the devil left him and, behold, **angels** came and ministered to him."

Angels with Jesus in the desert by James Tissot

John 5:4 (NASB) speaks of the healing waters at the pool in Bethesda that "from time to time an **angel of the Lord** would come down and stir up the waters."

An angel comforts Jesus Christ during His agony in the garden before he is seized and imprisoned by the Romans. Jesus himself sees an angel. Luke 22:43 (NIV) states, "And He had sight of an angel from heaven, encouraging Him."

An angel comforting Jesus in the Garden of Gethsemane by Carl Heinrich Bloch (1865–1890)

In Matthew 28:3–5, Mark 16:6–7, John 20:11–13, and Luke 24:5–7 (NASB), an **angel of the Lord** speaks at the empty tomb, following the resurrection of Jesus and the rolling back of the tombstone.

Angel at the tomb of Jesus Christ

And behold, there was a great earthquake, for an angel of the Lord descended from heaven and came and rolled back the stone and sat on it . . . the angel said to the women,

"Do not be afraid, for I know that you seek Jesus who was crucified. He is not here, for he has risen, as He said. Come, see the place where he lay. Then go quickly and tell his disciples that he has risen from the dead, and behold, he is going before you to Galilee; there you will see him. See, I have told you."[31]

The Resurrection Angel in blue

31 . Gospel written by Matthew, chapter 28, New King James Version (NKJV).

The Resurrection Angel in bright white

Printed in the United States
by Baker & Taylor Publisher Services